Bicycles and Motorcycles

June Loves

Chelsea House Publishers
1974 Sproul Road, Suite 400
Broomall, PA 19008-0914

The Chelsea House world wide web address is www.chelseahouse.com

Library of Congress Cataloging-in-Publication Data Applied for.

ISBN 0-7910-6591-X

First published in 2001 by
Macmillan Education Australia Pty Ltd
627 Chapel Street, South Yarra, Australia, 3141

Copyright © June Loves 2001

Edited by Miriana Dasovic
Text design by Anne Stanhope
Illustrations by Lorenzo Lucia, Tech View Studio
Photo research by Legend Images
Printed in China

Acknowledgements

The author and the publisher are grateful to the following for permission to reproduce copyright material:

Cover: BMX National Championships, Melbourne, 1984, courtesy of Coo-ee Picture Library.
Australian Picture Library/L. Meier, p. 14 (left); Australian Picture Library/Photoedit, p. 13 (bottom); Coo-ee Picture Library, pp. 5, 7 (left), 8, 9 (top), 10-11, 15, 19 (left); Digital Vision, pp. 25 (left), 27 (bottom); Great Southern Stock, pp. 14 (right), 18, 20-1, 22, 23, 24, 25 (top), 28; Honda Motorcycles, p. 19 (right); Legend Images, p. 29 (bottom); Jiri Lochman/Lochman Transparencies, p. 29 (top); Mary Evans Picture Library, pp. 6, 7 (right), 16; Photodisc, p. 9 (bottom); Tom Putt, Sport the Library, p. 26; Dennis Sarson/Lochman Transparencies, p. 27 (top).

Check the screen on each double-page spread.

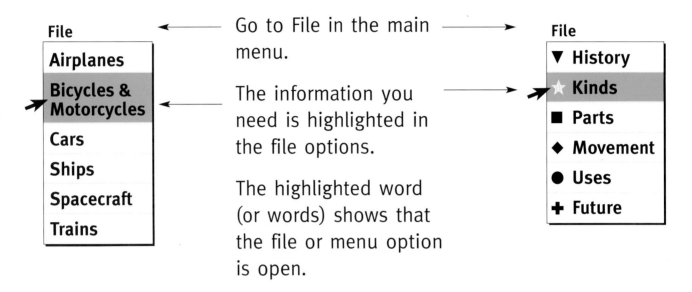

Go to File in the main menu.

The information you need is highlighted in the file options.

The highlighted word (or words) shows that the file or menu option is open.

The highlighted icon at the bottom right of the screen tells you what information is on that page.

A horizontal arrow beside the page number shows that the topic runs over the double-page spread.

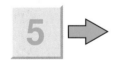

A vertical arrow beside the page number shows that the menu option is completed.

This hand icon beside an underlined word in bold shows that the word also appears in the glossary on page 31.

File 1

The word bicycle means 'two wheels'. A bicycle is a simple machine with two wheels. It is an easy machine to ride and provides a cheap and quick way to travel.

In many countries, bicycles are the main form of transportation for people and goods. Bicycles are often called bikes.

Bicycle power

Bicycles need 'people power' to make them go. The cyclist's legs and feet power the machine parts of the bicycle to make it move. A cyclist can usually travel twice as fast as a person who is running.

No pedals

Bicycles were invented about 200 years ago. The first bicycle was like a wooden scooter. It was invented in about 1790 by a Frenchman, Comte Mede de Sivrac.

The Draisine or 'dandyhorse' was an improved model invented in about 1817. These bicycles did not have pedals. The riders pushed themselves along with their feet, and the steering bar was connected to the front wheel.

Bone shakers

In 1839, the Scottish blacksmith, Kirkpatrick Macmillan, added foot pedals to the Draisine. These pedal-powered bicycles were called 'bone shakers' because the solid wheels gave the rider a bumpy ride!

The 'dandyhorse' did not have pedals.

The penny farthing bicycle

The penny farthing bicycle was invented about 1870. It had a huge front wheel and a tiny back wheel. These bicycles were named after two old British coins — the (big) penny and the (small) farthing. The rider turned the pedals on the front wheel to move the bicycle. Each turn of the pedal turned the large wheel around once. This made the penny farthing bicycles travel with greater ease than earlier bicycles.

The safety bicycle

The first 'safety' bicycle was produced by J. K. Starley of England in about 1885. It was similar to modern bicycles and safer to ride than high-wheeled bicycles. The safety bicycle had two wheels of equal size, brakes, air-filled tires, and was chain-driven.

Popular transportation

Bicycles became very popular in the 1800s. They changed from being a toy for rich people to become a cheap and reliable form of transportation for everyone. However, they lost their popularity in the 1900s as the motor car was developed.

Some models of the penny farthing had a front wheel about 1½ meters (5 feet) high.

The 'safety' bicycle, 1885.

THE ROVER SAFETY BICYCLE (PATENTED).

Safer than any Tricycle, faster and easier than any Bicycle ever made. Fitted with handles to turn for convenience in storing or shipping. Far and away the best hill-climber in the market.

MANUFACTURED BY

STARLEY & SUTTON,

METEOR WORKS, WEST ORCHARD, COVENTRY, ENGLAND.

Bicycles are made in many different styles and shapes to suit the needs and sizes of riders.

Road bikes

Road bikes are made to ride on paved roads or streets. They are the main form of transportation in some countries.

BMX bikes

BMX bikes have small wheels and very strong frames. The wheels have wide tires with deep **treads** that provide grip on slippery and rough dirt tracks.

BMX riders can do all sorts of stunts on their bikes.

Taxi bicycles

Some bicycles, such as rickshaws and trishaws, are used as taxis or pedicabs. Passengers pay the rider to carry them to their destination. Trishaws have three wheels. The rider can sit in front or behind the hooded carriage, which can transport passengers or goods.

Unicycles

Unicycles have one wheel and no handlebars to hold. This makes them difficult to ride. Clowns and other ☞ circus performers can **balance** on unicycles while they juggle or perform other tricks.

Racing bikes

Racing bikes are designed to move fast. Their frames and wheels are made of tough, lightweight materials. The wheels often have solid discs instead of spokes to reduce air resistance.

Mountain bikes

Mountain bikes are designed for riding over steep and rough surfaces. They have sturdy frames, flat handlebars ☞ and wide tires. They have **gear** systems with 21 speeds, and are often made with front and rear spring systems which cushion the riders against road bumps.

Pedicabs are a popular form of transportation in many parts of Asia.

A unicycle has only one wheel and no handlebars.

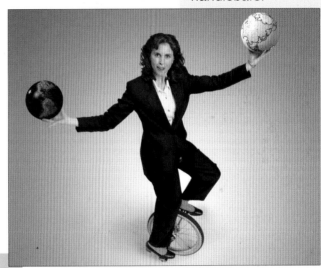

Tandem bikes

The tandem bike is built for carrying two riders. One rider leads and steers, but both riders pedal the bicycle.

Tricycles

Tricycles have three wheels and are very easy to ride.

Parts of bicycles

File 1

| Bicycles |
| ▼ History |
| ★ Kinds |
| ▇ Parts |
| ◆ Movement |
| ● Uses |
| ✚ Future |

Parts of a modern bicycle

The basic design of bicycles has changed little since they were invented in 1839. Small changes have been made to the shape of the handlebars, the size of the wheels, and the materials used to build the bikes.

tires – made of an outer tube of strong rubber and an inner tube which is blown up by a pump. The surface of a tire is called its tread. The invention of inflatable tires in 1888 made cycling more comfortable

gears – make it easier to ride uphill as well as enabling the cyclist to go faster on a hill. The cyclist operates the gears from the handlebars

saddle – the seat for the rider

wheels – can vary in size according to the type of bicycle and size of the rider. Bicycle sizes are based on wheel sizes. Road bikes can have 650, 675 or 700 millimeter (26, 27 or 28 inch) wheels.

brake blocks

chain wheel and rear **sprocket** – these act like pulleys connected to a belt (chain). The chain drives the back wheel

frame – made of hollow tubes of light steel or metal alloys

brake levers – most bicycles have calliper brakes which stop the bicycle by pressing two brake pads against the rim of the wheel. The cyclist stops the bike by pulling the brake levers on the handlebars. Some bicycles have back-pedal brakes. The cyclist stops the bike by pushing backwards on the pedals

brake cables

handlebars – can be curved downwards or upwards. Grips on the handlebars stop the rider's hands from slipping

drink bottle holder

COLNAGO

pedals – are connected to the back wheel by a chain

spokes – thin rods or wires connect the hub of a wheel with the rim. They strengthen the wheel without making it heavy

Movement of a bicycle

How a bicycle works

The sprocket wheel is joined to the back wheel. The chain fits over the teeth of the chain wheel. When the rider pushes the pedals, the chain wheel goes around. As the chain is pulled around, it turns the sprocket wheel. The sprocket wheel turns the back wheel and this pushes the bike forward.

How bicycle brakes work

A bicycle brake uses the <u>friction</u> between a hard rubber pad and the metal rim of the wheel to stop the movement of the wheel. A cable joins the brake to the brake lever. When the brake lever is squeezed, another set of levers presses pads against the rim. This slows or stops the wheel.

A clean way to travel

Bicycles are an environmentally-friendly form of transportation because they do not create <u>pollution</u>. Many countries encourage people to use bicycles to reduce pollution levels.

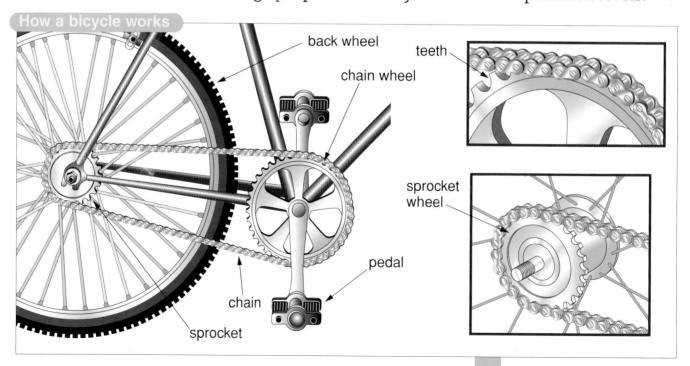

How a bicycle works

back wheel
chain wheel
teeth
sprocket wheel
pedal
chain
sprocket

brake pads

brake cables

brake levers

bike pads
apply friction
here

pedal

friction here makes the
bicycle go forward

Safety regulations vary across the country,
but wearing a helmet when riding a bicycle
always makes good sense.

Riding a bicycle

Cyclists ride bikes by balancing on two wheels and steering with the handlebars. They push the pedals with their feet to make the wheels go round. This moves the bike. Cyclists need to concentrate on the road ahead and the traffic around them.

The bicycle must keep moving forward for the cyclist to continue riding it. If the bike stops moving, it will fall over unless the rider supports it with a foot on the ground.

Riding BMX bikes

BMX riding is a popular sport. Riders race over dirt or grass tracks and the course is full of sudden twists and bumps. Riders can do exciting stunts on their bikes, such as 'wheelies' and jumps.

Bike safety

Cyclists need to wear safety helmets and protective clothing. They need to know and obey the road rules so they can be safe when riding in traffic. For example, cyclists must signal before turning a corner or stopping.

Uses of bicycles

File 1

- **Bicycles**
- ▼ **History**
- ★ **Kinds**
- ■ **Parts**
- ◆ **Movement**
- ● **Uses**
- ✚ **Future**

Bicycles can be put to many different uses.

Travelling to work and school

In many cities the roads are crowded with cyclists travelling to and from work and school.

Delivering mail

Postal workers use bicycles to deliver parcels and letters in many cities and towns.

Using a bicycle makes the job of delivering mail quicker and easier.

Bicycles are more popular than cars in Beijing.

Recreation and exercise

Many people enjoy riding bicycles for recreation and exercise on specially made bicycle tracks in cities and towns.

Bicycle racing

Bicycle racing is a popular sport. Individual or team riders race on indoor or outdoor tracks.

Sprint races

Sprint races are short races which take place in a stadium called a **velodrome**. The riders race around an oval track. The oval track is **banked** to stop the bikes from skidding on the bends.

Long-distance road races

Long-distance road races are held outdoors between towns or around a course. The Tour de France is a famous bicycle marathon through Europe. It lasts about 24 days and covers around 4,000 kilometers (2,486 miles). Teams of riders compete in the race as they cycle a route that includes a climb into the French Alps.

Mountain bike racing

Mountain bike racing is a thrilling sport. Cyclists ride their strong, reinforced bikes over rough terrain that includes hills and sharp turns.

A cyclist races on the banked track of a velodrome.

Motorcycles, or motorbikes, are bicycles that are powered by an engine located between the front and back wheels. Motorcycles can travel at much faster speeds than bicycles. They are not as cheap or simple to use as bicycles, but they are cheaper to run than cars.

Motorcycle power

An engine gives a motorcycle its power to move. Some motorcycles have very powerful engines. They can reach speeds of 260 kilometers (162 miles) per hour or more. Other motorcycles, such as mopeds, have very small engines. They may even need to be pushed uphill.

Early motorcycles

In 1868, two French brothers, Ernest and Pierre Michaux, fitted an engine onto a bicycle. They used a steam engine to power their bicycle. It worked but was not a great success.

In 1885, a German engineer, Gottlieb Daimler, built a bicycle fitted with a gas engine. The bicycle worked but it looked big and clumsy. It could move only slightly faster than a person could walk. This early motorcycle had wooden carriage wheels with iron rims.

Motorcycles continued to be developed, but did not become useful vehicles until the 1900s.

The Benz motor-tricycle, 1885.

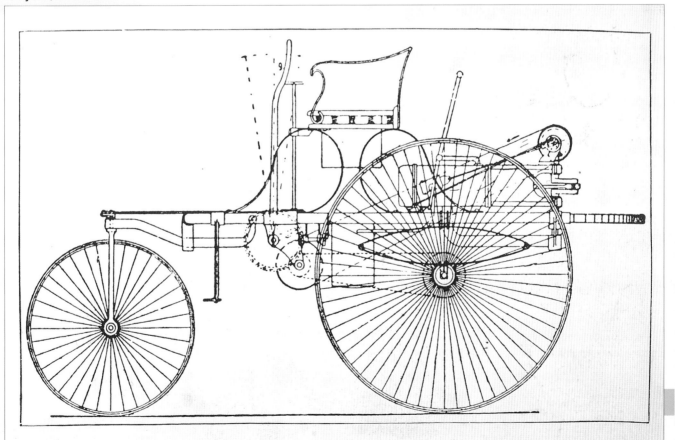

Kinds of motorcycles

Different kinds of motorcycles are designed for different uses. Motorcycles are grouped by engine size, which is usually measured in cubic centimeters, or cc. Racing motorcycles usually have bigger engines than motorcycles that are used for travelling on roads.

Mopeds

A moped is the simplest kind of motorbike. It has a two-stroke engine that is never larger than 50 cc.

Harley Davidson

The American Harley Davidson motorbike is a famous top-of-the-range motorbike with a four-stroke engine. Recent models have a five-speed transmission, disc brakes and an engine set on rubber.

The Harley Davidson is a luxury motorcycle.

ATVs

ATV stands for 'all terrain vehicles'. These are three-wheeled motorcycles with wide wheels which help to balance the bike.

Trail bikes

Trail bikes are made for riding over rough terrain such as dirt trails and rough tracks. Riders can compete against each other over a marked course.

Superbikes

Superbikes can perform as well as Formula One racing cars. The Japanese Super Blackbird is built by Honda. It has a speed of 300 kilometers (186 miles) per hour and can accelerate from 0 to 96 kilometers (60 miles) per hour in only 2.5 seconds.

Sidecars

Some motorcycles have sidecars which are designed to carry extra passengers. Motorcycles with sidecars are also used for racing.

Choppers

Choppers are motorcycles that are made by their owners. The owners 'chop' the design around and make motorcycles with features to suit themselves. Some choppers look very unusual.

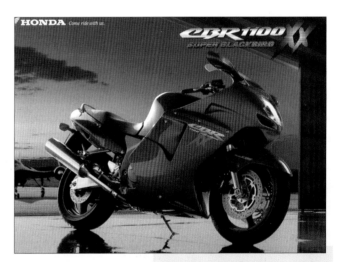

The Honda Super Blackbird is designed for racing.

Trail bikes are designed for riding under harsh conditions.

Motorcycles are made up of hundreds of different parts, big and small. Each part is important in making the motorcycle work. The parts can be grouped into systems — fuel, brakes, transmission, suspension and ignition. These systems work together to make the motorcycle go.

saddle – the rider's seat with space for one passenger to sit behind the rider

suspension – a system of springs which act like a cushion and create a smooth ride. A motorcycle has two suspension systems, one at the front and one at the back

transmission – this holds a collection of tooth-edged wheels that can be linked together in different ways. These gear wheels change the speed of the engine into a faster or slower drive at the rear wheel

exhaust pipe – waste fumes that are released by burning fuel escape from the engine through here

rear brake – the right foot operates a brake on the rear wheel. Most motorcycles have disc brakes on the front wheel. These also help to slow the bike down

fuel tank – holds the fuel that powers the engine

Handlebars – used for steering

throttle – when the throttle is twisted back, more fuel is released into the engine

front brake lever – operates the brake on the front wheel

mudguards – stop mud and water from splashing onto the rider

frame – supports the engine and other parts of the motor-cycle. It is made of lightweight metal

engine – this is fitted in the frame between the two wheels

The four-stroke engine of a motorcycle.

Motorcycle engines

Motorcycle engines normally work with pistons. Pistons are metal tubes that move up and down inside a hollow cylinder. This movement turns the crankshaft. Motorcycles usually have two- or four-stroke engines.

Two-stroke engines

In a two-stroke engine the piston moves up and down twice in each cycle. Most early motorcycles had two-stroke engines. Some smaller motorcycles still use them.

Four-stroke engines

Some motorcycles run on a piston engine that uses four strokes to produce power. Four-stroke engines are more complicated than two-stroke engines. They also have more working parts and produce more power.

Braking

Motorcycles must have a good braking system because they travel very fast. Most motorcycles have two separate braking systems. The disc brake on the front wheel is operated by the rider's hand on the brake lever. The drum brake is on the back wheel and is operated by the rider's feet.

Tires

Tires give the motorcycle good grip on the road and help the rider to control the motorcycle. Tires have different rubber patterns, called treads. Different treads are suited to travelling on different surfaces.

Radial tires

Radial tires have channels cut into the rubber to form a tread. This tread helps the tire to grip the ground. Rain and other water is drained away by the channels in the tread.

Slick tires

Slick tires have a smooth tread. They grip the road well because more of the tire surface touches the ground. Racing motorcycles use slick tires when the course is dry.

Slick tires work best in dry weather.

Radial tires are best in wet weather.

File 2

Riding a motorcycle

To ride a motorcycle, the rider uses both hands and feet. The motorcycle rider has to remain balanced when travelling at speed, especially when turning a corner or riding over difficult roads. As well as balancing on a motorbike, the rider must control the speed and change gears. The rider controls the motorbike through the instruments on the panel. Riders must also concentrate on the road and traffic around them.

Motorcycle instruments

dials – for speed, pressure, temperature, oil and fuel

switches – for lights and indicators

ignition lock and switch – start the engine

Cornering

Motorcycle riders need to lean into the corner of a bend to keep their balance when travelling at speed. A rider must learn how far to lean into a bend before the motorcycle's balance is upset. Even experienced riders can fall and hurt themselves.

Motorcycle safety

☞ Riders wear **crash helmets** with plastic
☞ **visors** to protect their heads and faces. They also wear protective clothing. In most countries a person must pass a driving test to gain a license that allows them to ride a motorcycle on the road. They have to demonstrate their skills in handling a motorcycle, as well as their knowledge of the traffic laws.

Motorcycle riders wear protective clothing.

Motorcycle racers are experts at rounding corners at high speed, but every motorcycle rider must learn how to lean into a bend without falling off.

Movement of motorcycles

In sidecar racing, the passenger leans out to balance the bike around corners.

Motorcycle racing

Racing motorcycles compete in classes according to their engine size. There are different kinds of races for different styles of motorcycles. Racing motorcycles are designed to be streamlined so they can go faster. They are lighter than ordinary motorcycles and have wider handlebars and thinner wheels. Racing motorcycles use slick tires with no treads.

Speedway racing

Speedway racing is a popular sport. The motorcycles have no brakes or gears. The riders uses their feet to control the bike as they go around corners. Most riders use special footgear such as steel-capped shoes.

Sidecar racing

In sidecar racing the rider drives the motorcycle and the passenger sits in the sidecar. As they go around corners, the person in the sidecar leans out to balance the bike.

Motorcycle circuit racing

Motorcycle races are held on circular racing tracks or circuits all over the world. The most important are the Grand Prix races which are held in different countries. The rider who wins the most races becomes the world Grand Prix champion.

Riders compete in the Australian Motorcycle Grand Prix.

Riders need a lot of skill to control their bikes when racing in a motor cross competition.

Cross-country racing for motorcycles

This sport is known as motor cross or scrambling. It is a popular form of motorcycle competition. Tough, lightweight motorcycles are specially made to race over rough ground. They have a raised body, knobby tires and a strengthened suspension. The motorcycles often skid or leap in the air as they travel over mounds and other obstacles.

Dragster racing

Dragsters are the fastest motorcycles today. They race in straight lines because they move at such high speeds. The crouched position of the rider helps to streamline the bike.

Motorcycles are a popular form of transportation. They have many uses because they can travel fast and use less fuel than cars. They are also used for recreation and sport.

Policing

Police officers use motorcycles in their work. Motorcycles can move easily through traffic to reach an emergency. Motorcycles also make good pursuit vehicles because they are fast enough to overtake most cars on the road.

The police also provide motorcycle escorts for ambulances and official cars for important people such as prime ministers and presidents.

Police motorcycles are fitted with two-way radios to keep police in touch with their stations. They also have sirens and flashing lights to warn people that police are approaching.

Motorcycles can be used to round up sheep and cattle, as well as helping in other tasks.

Agriculture

Farmers often use motorcycles to help them with their farm work. Farmers often use ATVs because the wide wheels give good balance when travelling over rocky and uneven ground.

Medical emergencies

Motorcycles are used by medical workers for emergencies because they can weave in and out of the traffic to arrive at an accident quickly.

Delivering messages

Some motorcycles are used by couriers to deliver messages, official documents and parcels. Courier motorbikes offer fast and reliable services to people.

Couriers use motorcycles to deliver documents.

Bicycles and motorcycles will continue to improve as designers take advantage of the latest developments in materials, design and electronics.

Motorcycles are being designed that can adjust to the size and riding position of the rider. They can even change color with the light, so the rider remains visible at all times.

Electric-powered bicycles may become a common sight on our roads. Bicycles with carrying attachments could be used as taxis and to provide light towing services.

Transportation glide systems may be common sights in our cities and towns in the future. When cyclists travel on these moveable pathways, they will be able to move at 10 kilometers (6 miles) an hour faster than they would riding their bicycles outside the systems.

A transportation glide system.

Glossary

balance — to have equal weight on each side or to keep the bike steady.

banked — sloping sideways. A banked track helps to keep the bike under control.

crash helmet — a padded helmet worn by cyclists and motorcyclists to protect their heads.

friction — the force that is produced when two objects rub against each other. It slows down any movement and stops sliding.

gears — a set of toothed wheels that helps a bike to change speed.

pollution — substances that spoil our surroundings and may damage our health.

sprocket — a small wheel with teeth to catch on a chain.

treads — the patterns on a tire that help it grip the surface of the road.

velodrome — an arena with a banked track, for bike racing.

visor — the front part of a crash helmet which covers the rider's face.

Index